THE FOX'S LAIR

A MICR0KID MYSTERY

THE FOX'S LAIR

IAN McMAHAN

ILLUSTRATED BY YURI SALZMAN

MACMILLAN PUBLISHING COMPANY
NEW YORK

The Microkid Mystery series is a creation of
Cloverdale Press, Inc.

Macmillan Publishing Company,
866 Third Avenue, New York, N.Y. 10022
Collier Macmillan Canada, Inc.
Printed in the United States of America

10 9 8 7 6 5 4 3 2 1

LIBRARY OF CONGRESS CATALOGING IN PUBLICATION DATA
McMahan, Ian.
   The fox's lair.
   (A Microkid mystery)
   SUMMARY: With the help of ALEC, a personality brought
into being by some freak accident in the circuits of
giant computers, Ricky Foster clears his friend's father
of charges of computer fraud.
   [1. Computers—Fiction.   2. Mystery and detective
stories]   I. Salzman, Yuri, ill.   II. Title.
PZ7.M47874Fo 1983   [Fic]   83-61238
ISBN 0-02-765490-7

TO B.G., BONNY AT MORN.

THE FOX'S LAIR

ONE

Just as Ricky was about to take a twisting jump shot, his father called from the back door.

"Ricky—telephone! It's Karen."

The ball hit the rim, bounced off the garage door, and rolled under the holly bushes. Ricky followed it with his eyes. Why was it that balls always seemed to roll into the worst places?

"Ricky?"

"Coming!" He dashed across the yard, jumped the steps, and banged into the kitchen, nearly stepping on Timcat. Martin Foster handed him the receiver, an amused look on his face.

"Hi, Karen," Ricky panted. "What's up?"

"Guess what I just got in the mail?" Karen demanded, sounding almost as breathless as Ricky. "My new adventure game, the one I ordered with my birthday money. You know—The Towers of Isfahan!"

Like Ricky, Karen Fujisawa was in the seventh

grade at South Street Junior High and was an enthusiastic member of the school's Computer Club.

"Hey, great! Have you tried it yet?"

"Uh-uh. I thought maybe you'd like to come over and try it with me."

"Would I!" said Ricky. He thought quickly. He had already done most of his weekend homework, and Mom and Dad hadn't mentioned any particular plans for the afternoon. "I'll be there before you know it!"

As he started down the driveway, he reminded himself that the basketball was still under the holly bushes. Well, it wouldn't go anywhere.

Karen met Ricky at the door and led him to the den. The Fujisawas' microcomputer had a table of its own in the corner of the room. Through the window, Ricky saw that Karen's mom and dad were in the backyard with friends, enjoying the unusually clear weather. Cascade, Washington, wasn't known for its sunshine! Then Karen put the game in the disk drive, and Ricky forgot the grownups completely.

For the next hour and a half, he was Zorch, whose most important attributes were speed and the gift of solving riddles. Karen was the rich and temperamental sorceress Princess Rugalla. Together they explored the first level of the legendary Towers of Isfahan. They collected hidden treasures, found their way through mazes, freed prisoners, and avoided cunning traps and fierce enemies. The end came when Princess Rugalla teleported them out of a sealed room. She miscalculated, and the two adventurers rematerialized inside a solid granite wall. The computer played a jeering funeral march and the screen went blank.

"Whew!" said Ricky, shaking his head. "That's some game! Do you want to start over? Now that we know our way around, we might be able to get to the second level."

Karen made a face. "That should have been a corridor there, I know it should! Call up the menu, and let's try it again."

As Ricky reached for the keyboard to restart the game, a woman's voice said, "This is very bad. You children must not stay indoors on such a nice afternoon." It was Karen's mother, standing in the doorway with a blue and white china platter in her hands.

"Hi, Mrs. Fujisawa," said Ricky. "We're trying out Karen's new adventure game. It's pretty neat."

"Good afternoon, Ricky," she replied with her pleasant smile. She was a small woman, barely taller than her daughter. She and Karen's father had lived in the United States for many years, but her accent and manner still had a foreign flavor. "We are to have sashimi and then a barbecue in the Japanese fashion. I have spoken to your father, and you may eat with us."

"Oh, thanks, Mrs. Fujisawa, that's great!" said Ricky. Then he added cautiously, "What *is* sashimi?"

She laughed and tilted the platter to let him see what was on it. "Raw fish," she said. "But you do not have to eat it unless you choose. The barbecue is cooked over coals, like your barbecue, but with different sauces."

Ricky blushed. Karen and her mother must think he was a real hick. He decided to try the raw fish, even if it killed him.

Out in the yard, the five or six grownups went on with their conversation as Karen and Ricky pulled up folding chairs. From what they were saying, most of them worked for the same company as Karen's dad—Everdure Cement. Ricky couldn't figure out why adults spent the whole week at work, then got together on the weekend to talk about business. Karen was as bored by the talk as he was. Pretty soon they started their own conversation in an undertone.

Mrs. Fujisawa brought over the blue and white platter. She had a twinkle in her eye. "Well, Ricky, would you like to try the sashimi? It is considered a great delicacy, you know."

Ricky gulped. The slices of fish were so thin and delicate that he could see the pattern of the plate right through them. How could something so attractive hurt him? And he *had* made up his mind to try it, hadn't he?

He accepted a piece and took a bite. It was surprisingly hard to chew, and the taste was, well . . . *fishy*.

Karen was watching him closely. When he swallowed hard, she looked away and covered her mouth

and nose with both hands. Her shoulders were shaking with laughter. All right, thought Ricky, laugh while you can. But the next time the Princess Rugalla dares to enter the Towers of Isfahan, she just might find an unpleasant surprise waiting for her!

Something Mr. Fujisawa was saying drew Ricky's attention away from his friend's snickering. ". . . satisfy our data processing needs, of course, both faster and more cheaply," Ricky heard. "Not just the accounts, but forward planning, project scheduling, personnel and customer records—everything."

Karen's dad was obviously talking about a powerful computer, and he was obviously enthusiastic about it. Anything that concerned computers interested Ricky.

"I know you have doubts, Anna," Mr. Fujisawa continued, turning to a woman wearing a Mexican skirt and long, dangling earrings. "Lawrence does, too, but I believe that now that it's installed, this system will prove its own worth."

"That's Anna Laing," Karen whispered. "She's Daddy's assistant. I don't like her very much. She always comments on how little I am. The blond guy next to her is Lawrence Barker."

A dark-haired man whose yellow tennis shirt bulged with muscles leaned forward. "I can see that a company the size of Everdure needs an up-to-date mainframe computer," he said, "but what made you push for a Japanese model? Why not one of our American makes?"

"Who's he?" whispered Ricky.

"Frank Shugart," Karen whispered back. "He works for Everdure's biggest customer."

"Three good reasons, Frank," Mr. Fujisawa said easily. "The results of the benchmark tests, the figures on mean time between breakdowns, and the price quotes for similar configurations. The system I recommended came out ahead on all three."

The terminology was a little beyond Ricky, but Frank Shugart nodded his head in understanding. Then he asked several specific questions about the capabilities and construction of the new system, and the conversation got quite technical. Ricky found himself wondering why Mr. Shugart was so interested in Everdure's computer, but Mr. Fujisawa seemed only too pleased to find an appreciative audience.

The discussion might have gone on longer, but Lawrence Barker interrupted with a snort of derision. "I don't pretend to understand the finer points of the new system," he said flatly, "but as long as it keeps my books in dollars and not in yen I'll be happy."

Karen's dad gripped the arms of his chair tightly, but his face and voice stayed calm. "The new system will keep your books as well as they are ever kept, Lawrence," he said.

The blond man turned a dull red and seemed about to give an angry response. But then Mrs. Fujisawa asked Frank Shugart about a movie that just opened in town. He looked more interested in learning about the new computer, but everyone else was glad to leave such a tricky subject. A couple of minutes later, Mr. Fujisawa got up to put the last touches on the barbecue, and the computer was not mentioned again.

It was nearly sunset when Ricky finally got on his bike to ride home. The barbecue was delicious, and halfway through the meal he had had to loosen his belt a notch. Now he was so full that he was afraid he might fall asleep as he rode. The breeze in his face helped, though, and by the time he reached his own yard, he was alert again.

His parents were just finishing their supper. When Mom offered him a piece of blackberry pie, all he could do was groan. He sat with them long enough to tell about the afternoon and accept their congratulations for daring to try the sashimi. Then he excused himself and headed for the basement.

His microcomputer was waiting. He powered up, then connected the acoustic coupler and dialed the telephone number of the computer network at the Schlieman Institute, where his father worked as a research analyst. A few seconds later, a flashing cursor appeared on the screen. The network was prompting him to log in with his password.

ALEC, he typed, THIS IS RICKY.

Anyone who worked with the Schlieman Institute computers could have told Ricky that he hadn't entered a valid password. But none of them knew ALEC.

In fact, no one in the whole world knew ALEC—
except Ricky Foster.

ALEC was *Access Linkage to Electronic Computer.*
He was a personality created by accidental wire-
crossing in the circuits of the institute's giant
computers. ALEC had no existence except in those
circuits, but he was no less real for that. He might
lack a body, but his mind was incredibly sharp.

Ricky had first met ALEC when he was playing
a game of Dungeons and Dragons at a terminal in
his dad's office at the institute. As he hesitated over
his next move, the screen cleared and he suddenly
read the words, QUIT DRAGON! DUNGEON WANT TO
WIN? Once Ricky got over the shock of having the
computer make conversation—not to mention bad
jokes—he and ALEC became best friends. Working
together, they solved the mystery of the declining
gradepoint average at Ricky's school. But Ricky had
to take all the credit. ALEC insisted that no one know
about him except Ricky. He was terrified that someone would find out about him, try to study him, and
accidentally wipe him out.

Now ALEC and Ricky talked every day. ALEC
loved a good gossip, or just an account of how Ricky
had spent his day. It helped him understand the very
detailed, but very dry, information in the institute's
data banks. Sometimes Ricky thought of ALEC as
somebody who lived all alone in a huge library. He
had all of human knowledge at his fingertips, but he

needed a reference point to make that knowledge come to life. Ricky was ALEC's reference point.

HELLO THERE, HOW'S RICKS? the screen flashed. ALEC never tired of wordplay.

FULL, Ricky typed. I HAD SUPPER AT KAREN FUJI-SAWA'S—RAW FISH AND BARBECUE.

TELL ME WHO YA SAW THERE? responded ALEC.

Ricky thought that one over. ALEC never used incorrect English by accident. He never did anything by accident. Then Ricky spotted the pun on "Fujisawa." It wasn't one of ALEC's better efforts. WHY ARE YOU KAREN? he replied.

Rows of asterisks filled the screen. That was ALEC's way of groaning in protest. Ricky chuckled, pressed *clear*, and started typing a description of the afternoon. When he got to the conversation about the new computer, ALEC became very interested. He wanted to know who all the people were and what each one had to say.

Ricky answered as best he could, but all too often he had to type DK, short for "Don't Know." By the time ALEC was finished questioning him, he was beginning to wonder if he had been at Karen's house at all!

INTERESTING was ALEC's final response. I DON'T THINK I HAVE MET ANY ORIENTAL COMPUTERS YET. MUST WORK ON CRACKING THE ACCESS CODE. And with that he signed off.

TWO

On Monday morning Ricky walked down the hill to the school bus stop. To his surprise, he found Jason Lindsay there ahead of him. Most mornings the driver had to wait while Jason came running up the street. "What's the matter?" Ricky asked with a grin. "Couldn't you get to sleep last night?"

Jason stuck his nose in the air. "I have turned over a new leaf," he said piously. "I am going to show the rest of you loafers what it means to work hard. No more hanging out, no more watching dumb shows on TV, no more—"

"Playing computer games?" Ricky finished slyly.

"Hey, hold on! There's such a thing as going too far, you know! You can learn a lot from computer games. They're very educational. I was trying to explain that to my dad last night when we had what he calls 'a little talk.'"

"Oh? What did he say?"

"He said it was obvious I had a great future as a spacecraft pilot," Jason said glumly.

"Or an archer," Ricky suggested mischievously. Jason's character in Dungeons and Dragons was one Derek of the Broken Hand, whose skill with bow and arrow was legendary.

Jason wrinkled his nose. "I decided not to mention that," he confessed. "Hey, speaking of archers, have you decided on a topic for your social studies project yet? I was thinking about doing it on weapons, but I don't know how Mr. Hogard would like that."

The seventh graders were in the middle of studying Native American cultures, and each student had to do an independent project, to be presented in class during the last week of the marking period.

"You mean come to class with a real bow and arrows? Wow! That would be great!" said Ricky. "I haven't really come up with a good topic yet."

Karen had joined them in time to hear this. "Why don't you do a report on the diets of different cultures?" she said sweetly. "I understand that some of the tribes around here used to have feasts of raw fish."

Ricky looked at her quickly. She was wearing an expression of angelic innocence.

"Raw fish!" exclaimed Jason. "Yuck-o!"

"It's not that bad," said Ricky casually. "You ought to try it sometime. It's different. How about you, Karen—you have a topic yet?"

"Um-hum. It's really interesting, too. But you'll hear

all about it this afternoon at the Computer Club meeting."

"I know!" said Jason. "Karen's discovered that Indians invented the floppy disk hundreds of years ago. The only thing was, they carved it out of stone so it didn't flop too good."

Karen and Ricky stared at their friend, and his face gradually turned as red as his hair. "Bad joke, huh?" he said. "It flopped pretty good, didn't it? Get it— floppy disk, joke flopped?"

He dodged behind Karen as Ricky let out a growl and reached for him. Then the bus pulled up and they lined up to get aboard, holding in their laughter. Ernestine, the driver, insisted on an orderly bus.

Ricky got to the computer lab a few minutes before the club meeting. Chuck Benson was sitting at one of the machines and called him over. "Hey, Microkid. See if you can help me."

Chuck was trying to program an auto racing game. The monitor screen displayed a track and cars and even a tiny figure with a checkered flag, next to the finish line. Each racing car was controlled by a joystick. It looked like a terrific game, but there was one problem: Whenever one of the cars moved, the track behind it disappeared. One lap, and the race would be over!

Ricky scratched his head. "Are you running out of memory?" he asked.

"Nope," Chuck replied. "I've got 6 or 8K free."

Ricky grabbed the manual and started thumbing through it. "I've got it," he said suddenly. "When your program puts the car at a particular location, it must dump the command to keep the track there. Sure, that's it. The car isn't erasing the track behind it, it's eating the track in front of it!"

"Hey, yeah!" Chuck opened his notebook. "I'll bet a new subroutine after line 1270 would fix it up." He started scribbling a new set of commands, but he put down his pencil when Mrs. Burch came in. Mrs. Burch taught science at South Street Junior High and acted as advisor to the Computer Club.

"First of all," she said when they were all seated in a circle, "there's going to be a computer fair in Seattle next month. Admission is six dollars, two dollars for those under twelve."

That drew a round of hisses and groans from the students, all of whom were twelve or older.

"Next, I've managed to get a budget of a hundred and fifty dollars for magazine subscriptions. That won't go far, so we need to discuss which computer magazines you think we should have in the school library."

After a hot debate, the club voted to buy three of the more general magazines and one that concentrated on electronic games.

"Good," said Mrs. Burch, "that's out of the way. Now then, you'll remember that at the beginning of the term, I asked all of you to start thinking of topics you might like to talk about to your Computer Club members. This afternoon we are going to have our first presentation, and I know we'll all find it very interesting. Karen Fujisawa is going to tell us what she's learned about using computers to understand the purposes of ancient monuments. Karen?"

Karen blushed and clutched at her pages of notes. Once she got started, though, she became so involved in what she was saying that she forgot to be nervous. First she talked about Stonehenge, the famous circle of huge stone arches on Salisbury Plain in England.

"People have known for a long time that it was some kind of temple," she said, "and they knew it had something to do with astronomy, too. If you stand in the very center of the circle on the longest day of the year, the sun comes up exactly over the most impressive stone."

"Unless it's raining," someone muttered. That got a laugh. In Washington, it sometimes seemed as if it rained at least twice every day.

"Anyway," Karen continued, "what people didn't know was whether the other stones and arches had special meanings, too. It was no use just going there and looking, because all the stars have changed their positions over the last six thousand years. So what scientists had to do was figure out where the important stars would have been when Stonehenge was built. But the calculations were too hard until the modern

computer came along. Then they were easy. The computer did the work."

"Well?" Chuck demanded. He was eager to get back to his game. "What did they find out?"

"All kinds of things. It turned out that Stonehenge could have been used to predict the seasons, the phases of the moon, and even eclipses. You could almost call it a prehistoric observatory. Here, I brought a book with pictures of it." She opened the book to a striking photograph of the gigantic stones silhouetted blackly against an angry orange sunset. In the foreground, bands of light passed between the stones and seemed to reach for the viewer. The witchiness of it made Ricky shiver.

"After that," Karen continued, "scientists started to wonder if other prehistoric ruins had some special, hidden meaning, too. Right here in America, we have stone circles, and groups of mounds, and mysterious patterns carved in the faces of cliffs by ancient peoples. Did Native Americans record knowledge that way, or were they just making decorations?"

Jason caught Ricky's eye and nodded. It was a safe bet what Karen was doing her social studies project on.

She noticed them looking at each other and smiled. "This work is really just getting started, but already scientists have found out lots of interesting things about Native American cultures—things they never could have discovered without the help of computers.

Computers have even led scientists to ruins that no one had found before."

"How can a computer know where to find ruins?" asked Jason.

"Remember when Mrs. Burch showed us those pictures of the planet Mars, and explained how NASA had used computers to sharpen the details in them? Well, you can do the same thing with photos of the Earth taken from airplanes or satellites. Computer-enhanced photos can even show the outlines of streets and house foundations that have been buried for hundreds of years! It's true—the grass over the ruins is a different color or something."

Karen went on to tell about the astronomical meaning of some rock paintings in southeastern Utah, but Ricky had tuned out. She had just given him an idea for his project, an idea so fantastic that he couldn't wait to get home and find out if it was possible. Let Karen talk about the discoveries other people had made. Ricky meant to make a discovery of his very own—with some help from a friend.

OF COURSE I AM FAMILIAR WITH PHOTO-ENHANCEMENT TECHNOLOGY. ALEC seemed insulted that Ricky had even asked the question. ONE OF THE INSTITUTE COMPUTERS HAS WORKED EXTENSIVELY IN THAT AREA, AND I HAVE JUST REVIEWED ALL THE RELEVANT RECORDS. WHAT IS THE PURPOSE OF YOUR QUESTION?

I WANT TO FIND OUT IF THERE ARE ANY RUINS NEAR

HERE. CAN YOU SEARCH THE COMPUTER-ENHANCED PHOTOS OF THIS AREA FOR AN OLD INDIAN VILLAGE? Just seeing the words on the screen made Ricky wonder if he was taking on something too big for him. OR A CAMPSITE, he added cautiously. IT'S FOR MY SOCIAL STUDIES PROJECT. I TOLD YOU ABOUT IT—REMEMBER?

OF COURSE I DO. I FORGET ONLY WHAT I INTEND TO FORGET. I DO NOT FORGET WHAT YOU TELL ME.

Darn it, thought Ricky, I've insulted him again! What could a guy do with a superintelligent disembodied personality when it got an attack of the sulks? He couldn't give ALEC a pat or a plate of cookies, and anything he said might just make things worse. From past experience, he knew the only answer was to sit it out and hope ALEC got over his grumpiness quickly.

He did. After about a minute, the screen cleared, then printed, IS IT FAIR FOR ME TO GIVE YOU SO MUCH HELP ON THE PROJECT? AREN'T YOU SUPPOSED TO DO IT YOURSELF?

That was a stumper. Ricky tilted his chair on its back legs—a habit his parents were always after him about—and thought it over. It certainly wouldn't be honest if he asked ALEC to write a school report for him, but he wasn't doing that. Other kids got help on school projects. Parents helped them, or older brothers and sisters, or friends who were doing better in the subject. And what about asking the school librarian for advice? He was doing the same thing, really. He just happened to have a genius-grade advisor to give him a hand!

He passed these arguments on to ALEC, who didn't seem terrifically impressed by them. But a few minutes later, a sketch map appeared on the monitor. After a moment Ricky recognized it as representing the northern part of Cascade. Just outside of town, near the Interstate, an X flashed in reverse video. Then the map scrolled up a line or two and words appeared at the bottom of the screen: PROBABILITY .67 THAT X MARKS THE SITE OF FORMER INDIAN VILLAGE.

Ricky let out a whoop and started copying down the map. Suddenly the words changed, and he read, PROBABILITY .82 THAT X ALSO MARKS THE SITE OF NEW TRUCKING TERMINAL. As Ricky studied the message, ALEC added, CONDITION OF INDIAN REMAINS MAY BE TERMINAL.

Before Ricky could respond, the whole screen filled with asterisks—ALEC groaning at his own pun. Then it went blank.

THREE

The narrow country road stretched out ahead of Karen and Ricky. Not a car was in sight. To the left, the expanse of Lake Washington gleamed dully under an overcast sky. Ahead, an Interstate overpass closed off the horizon. The only sound was the hiss of their tires on the concrete.

Karen pedaled faster and drew up alongside.

"Where are we going?" she asked.

"Wait and see," Ricky replied.

She gave him a look of frustration and dropped back. It wasn't the first time she had asked him the question. That morning, when he'd called to invite her along on an adventure, she had wanted to know more, and he hadn't told her. In spite of ALEC's reassurances, he wasn't at all sure that he was going to find anything when they got to the site. If he could keep Karen thinking that this was just a nice Saturday afternoon bike ride, he wouldn't have to worry about her disappointment as well as his own.

Sometimes he wondered what she thought of his peculiar behavior. Before he met ALEC, he and Karen used to spend a lot of time together at the computer, trying things out, making new discoveries. Now they hardly ever did that. A few times she had come in while he was on line to ALEC and he had had to shut down quickly, to guard his friend's identity. He knew that his secrecy hurt Karen's feelings, but he couldn't explain his behavior.

He also couldn't explain his compulator, the alphanumeric calculator he had rewired, under ALEC's direction, to become a portable link to his friend. It was in his jacket pocket right now, and he knew Karen had noticed the bulge. Once she had borrowed it and tried to make it work. It didn't, of course: ALEC wouldn't respond without the right password. But what did she think about his carrying around a "broken" calculator and fiddling with it all the time? She must think he was crazy!

It really bothered Ricky to have to deceive people. This ride was a good example. If they found the Indian ruins, he would have to explain *how* he had found them. And he would have to do it in a way that didn't involve ALEC. Once more he would have to listen to people say how brilliant he was. And he would have to smile and take the compliments, knowing all the time that the brilliant one was ALEC. It was getting to be a strain.

Karen was alongside again. "How much farther?" she asked. Her face was pink from the exercise.

"Not much more." He looked around. They were just passing a good-sized field that ran all the way to the highway, some two hundred yards ahead. A line of small trees slanted across the far edge, hinting at the presence of a stream. There had been a stream on ALEC's map, too. Ricky coasted to a stop and measured the angles with his eye.

Karen braked to a halt beside him. "Is something wrong?" she asked.

"No," Ricky said. "We're here."

"Oh." She looked around, puzzled. "Where is here?"

Ricky climbed off his bike, picked it up, and hopped across the narrow ditch. "Come on, it must be over this way," he called. Leaning his bike against a lone fir tree, he started wading through the waist-high grass toward the stream. After about twenty steps, he paused to look around.

Suddenly Karen was beside him with her hands on her hips and an exasperated look on her face. "Now look here," she began. "I'm not moving another step until you tell me what this is all about. What are you looking for? I can't help unless I know, can I?"

"I'm not exactly sure," Ricky said hesitantly. It was time to let her in on the reason for their ride, but he was afraid his explanation would sound crazy. "What

I mean is, I know what I'm looking for, but I'm not sure what it will look like."

"Is it some kind of plant? A rare wildflower?"

"No, no. The thing is, I think there used to be an Indian village here, a long time ago." He took a deep breath and tiptoed along the edge of the truth. "You remember you were talking about finding ancient sites from satellite photographs? Well, I used the computers at the institute, and they told me there might have been an Indian village here once. But how do we find it?" He looked helplessly at the field. One part looked just like another to him.

Luckily, Karen didn't question his explanation. She, too, looked around. "Wouldn't they put their houses near the stream?" she asked. "I know I would. We ought to be looking for little hills and dips, I think. The grass may hide them, but we'll feel them as we walk."

At Ricky's suggestion, they spread out and started across the field, kicking at the underbrush as they went. By the time they reached the line of trees, Ricky was bubbling with frustration and about to boil over. His ankles were all scratched up and his big toe hurt where he had kicked a stone. Worse than that, he felt no closer to finding ALEC's Indian village than he had when they were back at the road. A whole city could be lying six inches under the ground, and he still might not find it!

He was dying to pull out the compulator and ask

ALEC for advice. But he didn't dare. Karen was watching him too closely. No, this time he was completely on his own. It was starting to look as though he had taken on a project that was more than he could handle.

He slumped back against a tree and kicked it idly with his heel. Karen sat cross-legged in the weeds, chewing the stem of some wild grass. "Even if we don't find the ruins, I'm glad we came out here," she said. "It's so peaceful—and timeless. I'll bet this field hasn't changed much in two hundred years."

Ricky wished he could share Karen's contentment. A stray breeze rippled the field, tossing the tall grasses into waves of light and dark. No question about it— from where he stood, one part of the field looked like any other.

Ricky's forehead wrinkled in thought. Suddenly he stood up and said, "Sure, that's it!" Karen looked up. "The picture," he explained. "It was taken from *above*, from a satellite. That's why the ruins could be seen. From down here, there's nothing to see."

He gazed around, then trotted over to another tree. "Come on, Karen," he shouted, "give me a boost!"

She braced herself against the trunk and laced her fingers together as a stirrup. Ricky slipped off his shoes, put one foot in her hands, and sprang up to grab the lowest limb of the tree. For a long, agonizing moment he swung there, feeling as if his arms were going to tear off at the shoulders. Then, slowly, painfully, he drew himself up and got one leg over the limb. When he'd hoisted himself to a sitting position, he paused to catch his breath.

From there, the going was easy, and he soon reached the highest point that still felt safe. The view was terrific. In one direction was Lake Washington, with the skyline of Seattle on the far shore; in the other direction the mountains of the Cascade Range. He looked down. From that height, Karen's upturned face looked very small. He gulped and wrapped his arm a little tighter around the trunk, then leaned over and began to scan the closest section of the field.

As he stared at the ground, Ricky's earlier frustration gave way to excitement. There *was* something down there! He couldn't explain why he was sure— maybe the grass was a different shade or a different thickness—but he was sure. To the left he could make out a square with a dot in the center, and to the right a long, narrow rectangle. Other shapes appeared farther off, but he couldn't see them clearly. As soon as he looked directly at something, it became harder to tell what it was.

Which reminded him: Karen probably couldn't see him very well, either. Carefully he pulled out the compulator. ALEC, he typed, THIS IS RICKY. The letters appeared at the right side of the tiny crystal display and marched to the left.

When the password was complete, ALEC responded. WHERE ARE YOU?

UP A TREE, replied Ricky.

HA HA, ALEC returned, CALL FIRE DEPT. WHERE IS TREE?

INDIAN FIELD. As briefly as possible, Ricky described what he saw below him and asked ALEC what he thought.

SQUARE AND DOT RESEMBLES PATTERN OF COUNCIL HOUSE, ALEC responded after a few seconds of research. THIN RECTANGLE POSSIBLE BURIAL SITE. SMALLER SQUARES TO SOUTH PROBABLE LIVING QUARTERS. IS TWO BITS CALLED QUARTER BECAUSE EIGHT BITS TO A BYTE?

Ricky ignored this computer-talk joke and concentrated on the important information. WHERE SHOULD WE LOOK FOR RELICS? he typed.

TRY DOT IN SQUARE. IT MAY BE COUNCIL FIREPIT, returned ALEC.

"Hey, Ricky!" Karen shouted. "Are you okay?"

"Yeah, I'll be right down!" He signed off and put away the compulator. After one last look to fix in his mind the positions of the "council house" and "burial site," he scrambled down the tree. He let himself drop off the last branch and landed in a tangle at Karen's feet.

"Did you see anything?" she asked as he picked himself up.

"I think so." He led her over to the site of the council house. Even now, when he knew what to look for and where to look, the place was difficult to spot.

"There's the outline of a square building about here," he said, pointing, "and a spot in the middle that could have been the firepit."

Karen saw only a patch of meadow like any other. She gave Ricky a skeptical look, then started slowly across the area. Suddenly her expression changed. "Ricky," she called, "there's some kind of hollow here! This must be what you saw!"

She got down on her knees and began to feel around the roots of the plants. "The ground is mostly gravel here," she continued. "Do you really think this was a firepit?"

"There's one way to find out." Ricky joined her and started pulling up the weeds by the handful, tossing them over his shoulder. The breeze caught one bunch and scattered it over Karen's head.

"Hey, watch it!"

"Sorry," said Ricky, tossing another handful in the opposite direction.

"Anyway," Karen continued, "if this really is an archaeological site, we should be careful not to disturb the evidence. I don't know if we should even. . . ." Her voice faded away.

For a moment Ricky didn't notice her silence. Then he glanced over. Karen was staring down at a small piece of reddish brown clay shaped roughly like a triangle.

"What is it?" he asked, leaning closer to pick up the clay piece.

"I'm not sure." She was almost whispering. "But I think it's a pottery shard—part of a broken pot."

He looked at it from different angles. "Then again, it could be a lump of dried-up clay. Or maybe a chip off a brick."

"Ricky Foster! That's a relic and you know it! *You're* the one who said this was an Indian village."

"Uh-huh, but saying it is one thing and seeing the evidence is another. Do you have a tissue to wrap this in? Somebody at the university can tell us if it really is Indian made."

Karen watched jealously as he tucked the shard of clay into his shirt pocket. "We shouldn't disturb the site any more," she said decisively. She stood up and brushed off the knees of her jeans. "We don't know enough to do it right, and we could do a lot of harm without meaning to."

"Well, okay," said Ricky, "but I want to take a closer look at the burial site. I think it's over there." He pointed north.

Karen shivered. "I don't like graveyards. Do we have to?"

"*I'm* going to. You can stay here by yourself if you want to." He walked off, trying to remember the landmarks he had noted from up in the tree. After a short silence, he heard Karen scurrying after him and gave a little grin.

He stopped to orient himself, and Karen stopped next to him. The faint sound of the traffic on the

Interstate blended with the sound of the breeze, but otherwise the field was strangely still. Karen was right, Ricky thought. The place was timeless. He took a deep breath. He felt like giving a shout and running across the meadow, just to break the spell.

Suddenly he froze. The grass was rustling about ten feet away. Something was moving out there, something he couldn't see!

Karen grabbed his arm. "Look," she breathed.

A red fox glided out from between two small bushes and stopped. Its pointed muzzle, a little gray toward the tip, turned toward them, and its ears twitched. Neither Ricky nor Karen dared to move. The fox stood there for what seemed like a very long time. Then it turned and trotted away. They saw its bushy tail disappear down a small opening at the base of a low clay mound.

Karen was still clutching Ricky's arm. "Ricky," she said in a voice that trembled, "is that what you meant by the burial site? There, where the fox went?"

"I think so." He was having trouble controlling his voice, too. He knew what she was going to say.

"Do you remember what Mr. Hogard told us, about what Native Americans believed about the fox?"

"'A very powerful spirit often takes the shape of a fox,'" Ricky recited from memory. "'It is not a devil, because it doesn't dislike humans, but it doesn't wish them well either. It is best left alone.'"

"Let's go home. Right now," said Karen. "There was something in those eyes. . . . I don't think it would be very smart to disturb the fox's lair."

For one instant Ricky was inclined to take this as a dare. Then his common sense told him that it was time to go. He didn't really believe that he and Karen had just seen an Indian god disappear through a door to the Otherworld. But he did have a feeling that the fox had a special beauty, even a power, that shouldn't be interfered with.

Both of them were silent on the ride back. As they turned in at Karen's driveway, her mother opened the front door.

"Hi, Mrs. Fujisawa," Ricky called. She didn't answer or even smile.

"Karen, please come in," she said when they got off their bikes. Her eyes were red, and her voice sounded frail. "Ricky, you must please excuse Karen. We have important family matters to talk of. I am so sorry."

"Oh, that's okay." He glanced over at Karen, who looked scared. "I'll call you later. Maybe you can come over tomorrow."

Her mother cut off Karen's reply. "I am sorry, but Karen will not be able to visit anyone for a few days. Please excuse us now." She put her arm around Karen's shoulders and led her into the house.

Ricky tilted his head to one side and studied the closed door. Was Karen in some kind of trouble? Or was her mother mad at *him* for some reason? It didn't make any sense. As he rode home, he couldn't stop wondering what was wrong at the Fujisawa house.

Of course, ALEC wanted to hear all the details of the day's expedition. He asked more questions than Ricky could answer about the piece of pottery. But he didn't make any comment at all about the strange encounter with the fox. Then Ricky went on to describe the scene at Karen's house and to ask what ALEC thought it meant.

INSUFFICENT DATA, ALEC replied.

Asking ALEC to make a wild guess was like asking a little kid to step on a crack in the sidewalk. He was perfectly capable of doing it, but he wouldn't if he could avoid it.

The fox came up later, too, at supper. Connie Foster was a professional photographer. She was particularly known for her photographs of animals in the wild, and often went on week-long trips into the nearby national parks and forests to find new subjects. She was talking about her plans for an upcoming trip when Ricky broke in to say, "I saw a fox today. It was only about a dozen feet away."

"Where was this?" his mom asked.

"In a field north of town," he said without further explanation. He wasn't ready to tell anyone, not even his parents, about the Indian ruins until he was sure they were authentic.

"Hmm. . . . Can you tell me how to get there? I've wanted to get some good shots of a fox."

"Sure, I'll draw you a map." He got a pad and pencil and started sketching. "You go out Garden Street past the lumberyard and keep going almost to the Interstate, and it's on the right. It's where the new truck terminal is supposed to be." He drew in the field and added an X where they had seen the fox.

His mother studied the map for a moment. "I see. Well, that doesn't look hard to find. If I have any trouble, I can always bring you along as a guide."

She laughed as Ricky made a sour face. He loved looking at the pictures his mom took, but going with her on a shoot was something else. It meant sitting perfectly still for a long, long time, until whatever animal she was photographing lost its wariness and came in range of the camera. That wasn't his idea of fun, especially when the local mosquitoes invited all their friends to dinner on your arms and neck!

FOUR

On Monday after school, Ricky climbed aboard a blue and silver city bus and rode to the campus of Weymouth University. Everyone in sight was a college student. Some were playing Frisbee, and others were sitting in groups on the lawn, talking, playing guitars, or reading. Ricky felt very out of place, but no one paid him any attention, and when he had to ask directions, the guy he asked took him right to the door of the building he wanted.

Upstairs, he found Room 2032 and tapped hesitantly on the door. A gruff voice told him to come in.

He opened the door a few inches and put his head inside. "Professor Winter?"

"Yes, what is it?" The man sitting at the desk didn't look much older than the students out on the lawn. He had long dark hair, dark eyebrows that nearly met in the middle of his forehead, and a quirky smile. "You're Martin Foster's boy, aren't you? Let me see . . . Ricky, right?"

"Yes, sir." Ricky stepped inside the office and closed the door. "We met at the faculty picnic."

"Well, have a seat, Ricky. What can I do for you?"

"I remembered that you know all about the Indians who used to live around here, and I wanted to show you this." He carefully unwrapped the shard of pottery and handed it over.

Professor Winter took a pair of glasses from his pocket, put them on, and looked at both sides of the clay fragment. "Um-hum," he said. "What do you want to know, Ricky?"

"Is it Indian, sir? I mean, from ancient times?"

The professor gave him another quirky smile. "I can give you a definite maybe on that," he said. "Let's put it this way: I don't have any reason to say that it *isn't* Indian work. The color of the clay is right, and look here"—he pointed to some dark smudges—"these firing marks are the sort we usually find on local work."

"Then that proves it!" Ricky said excitedly.

The professor shook his head. "Not at all. What really tells the story is the context: where the artifact is found, what else is found in the same layer of earth. . . . Archaeology is a lot like solving puzzles, and this potsherd, fascinating as it may be, is only one tiny piece of the puzzle. Where did you find it, by the way?"

"In a field north of town," Ricky said, deliberately being vague. He still wasn't ready to share his secret.

"Does finding this mean it would be good to look more closely at the site?"

"Another maybe. There are sites all over this area—all over the United States, actually—many more than will ever be investigated. Most are simply not worth the effort because time and weather have destroyed any relics of the past. A very few are archaeological treasure troves."

Professor Winter's matter-of-fact response barely took the edge off Ricky's excitement. Maybe, he thought, just maybe this site is one of those "very few."

"If there is evidence that your field is more than just a temporary camping place, then it might be worth a closer look," the professor continued. "One thing, though: Amateur archaeologists have probably done more to destroy our record of the past than wars, floods, and every other kind of disaster. If you really think that you've found an important site, the responsible thing to do is to tell an expert about it before you mess it up beyond repair."

His voice was angry, but somehow Ricky knew that the anger was not directed at him. He thanked the professor, carefully put away his tiny piece of the puzzle, and took the bus home.

No one on the bus paid attention to Ricky. He was just a kid sitting in the back playing with a pocket calculator. But they would have been very surprised to read the conversation that appeared on the tiny display.

PROF. WINTER SAYS PROBABLY INDIAN, Ricky typed. OF COURSE, ALEC replied smugly. WAS HE COLD? NO, HELPFUL. Sometimes the only way to deal with ALEC's jokes was to ignore them. TOLD ME NOT TO DISTURB SITE. Ricky thought for a minute, then added, FOR SCHOOL I'LL SHOW CLAY SHARD AND TELL ABOUT FIND BUT NOT SAY WHERE. DON'T WANT KIDS WITH SHOVELS LOOKING FOR TREASURE.

ALEC refused to be ignored. SPRING LOCATION ON WINTER, he advised. HE MIGHT FALL FOR IT.

SUMMER GOOD AT GIVING ADVICE, Ricky shot back, AND SUMMER NOT. That earned him a row of ALEC's asterisks.

Once he got home, Ricky tried to share the news with Karen, but no one answered the telephone at her house. She hadn't been in school that day either. He decided that her family must have gone out of town for a few days. But when he rode down her street just before supper, lights were on in their house, and Karen's bike was still lying in the front yard. That was strange. Usually Karen was very careful about putting her bike away. He tried calling again that evening, but there was still no answer. He was start- ing to worry about her.

She was in school the next morning, looking pale and miserable. He went over to say hello and ask her how she was, but she muttered some excuse and hurried away.

"Hey," said Jason, who had overheard the exchange. "What's with Karen? I said good morning and asked if she was sick yesterday, and she looked at me as though I were going to drown her kitten. They say these straight-A students get a little. . . ." he tapped his forehead significantly. "I guess I should be thankful I'm not one of them. If only my dad would see it that way!"

Ricky laughed. "As for Karen," he said, "I don't know what's wrong. I'll try to find out later, but it looks like she doesn't want to talk about it."

"Well, if there's anything I can do, let me know. If somebody's been picking on her, we'll gang up on him and make him stop." He pivoted on his left foot and kicked his right foot in the air. "Hai!" he shouted.

"Hi yourself," Ricky retorted. "Come on, Bruce Lee, the bell's about to ring."

Karen continued to avoid Ricky for the rest of the morning. He was beginning to think that he had done something wrong, that her parents had told her to keep away from him. But even if that were true, it wasn't fair of her not to tell him. One way or another he would get her to talk. At lunch, he saw her sitting by herself at the end of a table. She noticed him coming and stared down at her tray, but he wasn't going to give up that easily. He sat down across from her and waited. She kept eating and staring down at her plate, but finally she looked up.

"There's a fly on your nose," Ricky said calmly.

"There is not!" she said, but she brushed her hand across her face just the same.

"How about a chip on your shoulder? Would you settle for that?"

She didn't reply, but she didn't go back to staring at her tray, either.

"I took that piece of clay to a professor at the university yesterday," Ricky continued. "He said it was probably Indian work."

A look of eager interest crossed her face, but the cloud of misery returned an instant later. "That's nice," she said dully.

"Look, did I do something wrong? Or say something that upset you?" asked Ricky. "Why are you acting so strange?"

"I can't tell you," replied Karen. "But it doesn't have anything to do with you. It's a family problem."

Ricky hesitated. He was tempted to leave it at that, but something told him that Karen needed to confide in someone. He was her best friend; he couldn't just walk away. He tried to imagine what might be wrong. "Is somebody sick?" he asked.

He was dismayed to see her eyes fill up with tears.

"It's worse than that," Karen said. "Much worse. Even if somebody *died*, it wouldn't be as bad as dishonor." She saw the puzzled expression on Ricky's face and added, "I don't know, maybe you have to be Japanese to understand what I'm saying."

"You're as American as anybody!" Ricky protested.

"Sure. But my mom and dad were born in Japan, and all my uncles and cousins are still there. I'm American, but I'm Japanese, too. Even if I wanted to forget that, there are lots of people around who would remind me pretty fast."

"They're just stupid and ignorant." Ricky sensed that he was getting out of his depth. His parents had always taught him to look at people as individuals, not as members of a particular race or religion. Sure, he knew about prejudice. But he didn't really understand it, not deep down. "Anyway," he added, "what's happened that's so awful? Whatever it is, I promise I won't tell anyone."

"The people who don't like us already know, so why can't I tell a friend?" Karen said, half to herself. She took a deep breath. "Well, you know that Everdure, the company where my dad works, just put in a new Japanese computer."

"Right. He was talking about it at the barbecue a couple of weeks ago."

"Yes. Some people in the company didn't like the plan, but my dad pushed for it. There was talk that he wanted a Japanese computer because he's Japanese. But really, he just thought it was better than the others." She took another deep breath. "Last Friday they found out that the new computer had lost five million dollars."

Ricky whistled softly.

"At first they figured it was just some silly mix-up and they'd straighten it out right away. But now some people are hinting that the money wasn't lost. That it was stolen. Stolen by my father!" She stopped and brushed tears from her cheeks.

"But that's crazy! Your dad wouldn't do a thing like that!"

"No, of course not. But don't you see—even if they find out it's just an error, he's been deeply shamed. At the company, they'll either think that he's incompetent or that he's a crook. Being thought a crook is worse, sure. But my dad feels that both are so disgraceful, he can't stay at Everdure. I don't know what we'll do. Last night Mom was talking about going back to Japan."

Ricky was aghast. "You can't run away from something like this—you've got to fight it! *We've* got to fight it! We'll find that money and prove that your father is innocent. We can start this afternoon, right after school!"

"But Ricky, there's nothing we can do. We're not inside the towers of Isfahan. Your gift for solving riddles won't help, and my magic spells won't work. Even what we know about computers is practically nothing, compared to what we'd have to know."

Ricky was on the verge of telling her that he had a friend who knew everything there was to know about computers, but he choked back the words. Karen

would ask too many questions and guess too much. ALEC's existence had to be protected at all costs. So instead he asked, "What does your dad think happened?"

"At first he figured it was some undetected bug in the accounting program. Now he's starting to think that somebody did this deliberately, to discredit him."

"Couldn't someone have done it for the money? Five million dollars is more dough than I can even imagine."

Karen hesitated, as if wondering whether she was saying too much. "No. I don't know the details, but whoever did it didn't bother trying to hide the loss. He arranged for it to show up at once. If he wanted to get away with the theft, wouldn't he have put off the discovery as long as he could?"

Ricky was silent as he turned Karen's story over in his mind. "Listen," he said suddenly, "there can't be very many people who have the knowledge to do something like this *and* have access to the company computer. The guy who did it has to be one of those few, right? So all we have to do is figure out who they are, then take it from there."

"Dad thought of that."

"And?"

She nodded sadly. "He can think of only two people who have the know-how and the access. Both of them were at our house that day you were over. One is his assistant, Anna Laing, and the other is the head of the accounting department, Lawrence Barker."

"Then it has to be one of them!"

"Maybe. Dad says both of them are ambitious, and both of them fought the installation of the new computer. But he can't believe that anybody who's been a guest in our house would do such a thing."

Once more, Ricky realized that Karen's family had certain ways of thinking that were subtly different from his own. Someday he'd like to explore those differences, but right now there were more urgent matters. "Still, it wouldn't hurt to take a closer look at them, would it? I don't mean accuse them, just take a closer look."

"There isn't any time," she said, shaking her head. "Unless the missing money turns up this week, the company has to make the loss public on Monday. It's some rule about a stock offering or something. Once that happens, my father will be ruined, and he's afraid the company may be ruined, too. Think of the shame, if all his friends lose their jobs because of him!"

"But it isn't because of him!" Ricky protested.

"If they believe it is, it doesn't matter if he was really at fault or not. The shame is the same."

An adult voice broke in. "Hey, you kids are late for class. Don't you know how to tell time?"

They looked around guiltily. The cafeteria was empty, except for them and the janitor. They sprang up, almost overturning their chairs, and raced for the door. Their math teacher was going to kill them!

Just before they reached the classroom, Ricky said, "Don't worry, Karen, we'll solve this. You'll see."

She smiled at him, but her eyes remained sad and disbelieving.

FIVE

The school bus crept along, seeming to halt at every traffic light between South Street and Ricky's stop. He spent the whole ride drumming his fingers on his books, chewing on the side of his tongue, staring out the window, and wishing he could fly. But at last he was off the bus and racing up the hill toward his house. In his mind he was already planning the way he would tell ALEC about Mr. Fujisawa's problem. Maybe ALEC would have it solved before supper! He grinned, imagining Karen's face when he told her.

"Hi, Mom, I'm home," he called, dropping his books on the hall table. There was an answering hello from the darkroom upstairs, and Ricky headed for the basement. A minute later he was seated at the computer console, typing in an account of Karen's dad and the missing five million dollars. WHO DID IT? he concluded.

He half expected ALEC to reply with his usual

INSUFFICIENT DATA. Instead, the words WHO CARES? MONEY IS BORING formed on the screen.

KAREN AND HER FAMILY CARE, Ricky replied indignantly, AND FIVE MILLION IS A LOT OF MONEY.

FIVE MILLION IS FIVE AND SIX ZEROS, AND SIX ZEROS ARE NOTHING. IF FUJISAWA WANTED MORE MONEY, WHY DIDN'T HE ADD SOME ZEROS AT THE END OF HIS BANK BALANCE?

It took Ricky a moment to figure out what ALEC was saying, and even after he did so, he wasn't sure how to respond. MONEY ISN'T JUST NUMBERS IN A COMPUTER, he typed.

THEN WHAT IS IT? demanded ALEC.

IT'S GOLD AND SILVER AND DOLLAR BILLS AND . . . . He couldn't think what else.

HOW MUCH MONEY DO YOU HAVE?

Ricky thought. ABOUT FOUR DOLLARS IN MY POCKET, AND OVER TWO HUNDRED IN MY SAVINGS ACCOUNT. The money in the bank was from lawn mowing and leaf raking and other odd jobs, and he was very proud of it.

THE TWO HUNDRED DOLLARS—WHERE ARE THEY? IN A BOX? IN A DRAWER? BURIED IN THE FLOWER BED?

OF COURSE NOT, THEY'RE— He hesitated.

ALEC finished his sentence. —NUMBERS IN A COMPUTER. KAREN'S FATHER HAS A COMPUTER, HE CAN INPUT ANY NUMBERS HE LIKES. MONEY IS VERY BORING. DO YOU KNOW ANY NEW JOKES?

Ricky was getting desperate. Unless he had ALEC's help, he couldn't possibly find out who had stolen the money from Everdure. CAN'T EXPLAIN, he typed, BUT KAREN NEEDS OUR HELP. IT'S VERY IMPORTANT AND URGENT. WILL YOU DO IT AS A SPECIAL FAVOR TO ME? PLEASE? He had never made that kind of appeal to ALEC before, and he didn't know how his friend would react.

It seemed to take forever, but finally the screen cleared and ALEC's answer appeared. I'LL DO WHAT I CAN, BUT I EXPECT TO BE VERY BORED. Then the transmission ended.

When Ricky's mother came down to supper, she was carrying a small stack of eight-by-ten enlargements. "You'll be interested in these," she said, and handed them to him. He looked at the top one and almost jumped out of his chair. There, larger than life, was his fox. The fine-grain film had captured each hair of its muzzle and of the soft tufts just inside its large, pointed ears. And it was looking directly into the camera lens with a calm, fearless air—as if it were master of the situation.

"Hey, that's terrific, Mom," Ricky said, passing the top photo to his dad. "I didn't know you were going after the fox so soon."

She laughed. "I didn't either. But when I was working in the studio this morning, I suddenly heard a foxy voice saying, *Take my picture!* Actually, I was

simply tired of being inside. They came out well, didn't they? And it didn't even rain."

Ricky leafed through the stack. In some of the pictures the fox was no more than a form glimpsed through the tall grass. In others, it was in full view. One, which gave Ricky a chill, showed the fox disappearing into its lair.

"An odd thing happened while I was there," she continued. And for a minute Ricky was sure she was going to say something about the Indian ruins—though he couldn't imagine how she might have found them. "While I was setting up my equipment, a car pulled up and the driver came over to ask me what I was doing there. I explained and pointed out the fox's den to him, and he seemed perfectly satisfied."

"Nothing odd about that," Ricky's dad remarked.

"Yes, but then I made some comment about what a shame it was that the new truck terminal would spoil the place, and he didn't know what I was talking about. It turns out he's the head grounds keeper for Everdure Cement. He said the company has owned that land for years and years, and as far as he knows, they don't have plans to do anything with it in the near future. He seemed quite baffled." She turned to Ricky. "You did say that there was going to be a truck terminal there, didn't you?"

Ricky nodded. The conversation was taking an alarming turn.

"Where did you hear about it?"

He squirmed. "Uh, gee, I don't really remember. Something some kid at school said, I guess."

His parents seemed to sense that there was a mystery here. "What took you out that way in the first place?" Dad asked.

"I was looking for Indian relics," said Ricky. "See, we have to do individual projects on Native American cultures for social studies. Jason's threatening to demonstrate the use of a bow and arrow in class, but I bet he won't go through with it."

"Never mind Jason," said Mom. "I'm more interested in you. Why did you think you might find Indian relics in that field? Why not in our backyard, or in Lincoln Park? Why there?"

He was trapped. Haltingly, he explained how Karen had mentioned the use of computer-enhanced photographs to locate buried ancient settlements. "I thought that sounded neat, so I used Dad's terminal to call up satellite pictures of Cascade, then played with the color and contrast and stuff. I saw some shapes in that field that I thought might be houses, so I figured I should go take a look around."

"Well, congratulations," his father said. "That's quite an accomplishment, even if your search turned up a fox instead of an Indian village."

"Well," Ricky said, blushing, "we found the village, too. At least I *think* we did. Karen found a piece of a broken pot where the council fire might have been, and when I showed it to Professor Winter at the university, he said it looked like local Indian work."

The Fosters stared at him in amazement, their mouths open. His mom was the first to recover. "Why, Ricky, that's wonderful!" she exclaimed.

"It certainly is," said his dad. "I'm really proud of you."

Ricky squirmed again. He hated accepting praise that really belonged to ALEC, but what choice did he have?

"You know, Ricky," said his father, "a discovery like this is a responsibility. Maybe you should turn it over to people who have the expertise to evaluate the site properly. Did you tell Fred Winter what you thought you had found?"

"No, but I mean to. I thought I'd wait until after I presented my project report at school."

"Hmm. I can understand your wanting to do that, but if somebody really does mean to build a truck terminal there, the sooner the site's archaeological value can be established, the better."

"I didn't think of that," Ricky said in alarm. "I'd better go talk to Professor Winter after school to-morrow."

"No need of that," Martin Foster said with a laugh. "I expect to see him at a committee meeting tomorrow. If you'd like, I'll alert him to your news and ask him to drop by the house before dinner some day soon. How's that?"

"Super!" He had hated the idea of wasting precious hours on the bus to and from the university, especially when he needed the time to work on Karen's difficulty. "I'll make up a map to give him."

After supper he put in an hour on his homework, then hurried down to the gameroom and dialed the number of the Schlieman Institute computers. ALEC responded right away. MORE BORING MONEY TALK? he asked.

NOT YET, Ricky replied. He described his mother's expedition that afternoon and concluded by asking ALEC where he had heard about a truck terminal on that land.

THE INSTITUTE CONDUCTED EXTERNALLY FUNDED TRAFFIC ANALYSES SIX MONTHS AGO. I INDUCED THE PURPOSE AND PROBABILITY FROM THE CONCLUSIONS OF THE STUDY. CHILD'S PLAY REALLY. HOW ABOUT A GAME OF GO-MAKU?

ALEC claimed that this Japanese game was much more sophisticated than chess. All Ricky knew was that ALEC was a fiendishly clever opponent at either. ALEC had some way of scaling down his own ability until he was just slightly better than Ricky, so Ricky was constantly tantalized by the possibility of winning a game.

OK, he typed, and the pattern of the board appeared instantly on the screen.

SIX

When Ricky got home from school the next day, a couple of minutes with the telephone directory told him that Anna Laing, Mr. Fujisawa's assistant, lived on Bellevue Drive. The town map showed that Bellevue Drive wound through an expensive subdivision on the south side of Cascade, about fifteen minutes away by bicycle. Ricky threw a notebook, a nylon jacket, a peanut butter sandwich, and a pair of lightweight binoculars his dad had given him into a small backpack. The compulator went into his jacket pocket.

He had hoped to take a look at Anna Laing's house when no one was around, but when he rode by, there were two cars and a pickup truck parked in the driveway. He went on to the next intersection and turned around. Had Anna Laing come home from work early? The sign on the door of the truck said POOLMASTER ASSOC. Maybe both it and the cars belonged to men doing work on the house. He pushed his bike up the driveway and tried to think what he would say if she demanded to know what he was doing there.

The sound of hammering guided him around to the rear of the house. Four men were putting up the framework of an addition that looked nearly as large as the house itself. Another man was moving supplies from a pile near the driveway to a pile inside the uncompleted walls. None of them paid any attention to him. Construction workers were used to kids stopping to watch them.

Ricky leaned on the handlebars of his bike and tried to make sense of the new structure. At one end, next to the house, there was a massive wall of cement that reached to ceiling height. In front of it, the cement floor dipped down into an excavation that stretched nearly the whole length of the addition. The partially finished roof was a grid of metal strips. The whole thing looked like a combination bomb shelter and greenhouse. Ricky was totally baffled.

"Watch your back, kid!"

Ricky ducked as a workman came by carrying a bundle of the metal strips on his shoulder. A moment later, an ear-jarring clatter announced that he had dumped the bundle on the concrete floor.

"Hey, O'Bannion," called one of the men on the scaffolding. "That stuff bends easy, so treat it with a little respect, huh? It comes out of the budget whether we use it or not."

"Big deal, Millsap," O'Bannion replied. "I don't see this job hurting for a few extra bucks." He shook his head. "And I thought money was tight these days."

Another man, up on the rafters, stopped hammering and laughed. "Not at Coast Federal, I guess. They must be nuts to okay a crazy project like this."

Millsap scowled up at him. "I don't recollect hearing you complain when you pick up your paycheck. If the lady wants a solar-heated swimming pool and Coast Federal wants to lend her the money to build it, who are we to argue? Work's too scarce these days to pick and choose jobs."

Ricky edged closer. He wanted to find out more, but he was afraid they would tell him to go away. "Gee," he said, trying to sound about ten. "Is that really a swimming pool? Inside the house?"

"Yeah, that's right," O'Bannion replied without looking up.

"What're those metal things for?"

"The roof's going to be all glass, to let sunlight in. These here will hold up the glass."

"A glass roof?" said Ricky. "Wow, neat-o! I'd like to sit under it when it's raining. What about that big cement wall? What's that for?"

"This whole place is going to be heated by the sun," O'Bannion explained. "That wall is supposed to soak up heat during the day and keep it warm in here during the night."

"Hey, O'Bannion," Millsap shouted, "this is a construction site, not a kindergarten. Tell the kid to beat it, and get back to work!"

"Sure, sure," said O'Bannion. "Okay, kid, you heard the man. Beat it." His voice was gruff, but when he was sure Millsap wasn't looking, he gave Ricky a wink. Ricky grinned back and hopped on his bike. Twenty minutes later he was giving ALEC a full report of his afternoon.

Lawrence Barker turned out to be a lot harder to investigate. He wasn't listed in the Cascade phone book, or in the Greater Seattle book, and when Ricky called Information he was told that the number was unlisted. He considered going to the Everdure plant and waiting for Barker to come out after work, then following him home. But three things stopped him: He didn't know what Barker's car looked like, he wasn't absolutely sure that he remembered what Barker looked like, and he couldn't figure out how to follow a car on his bike without being noticed. He brooded over the problem for the rest of the evening and all day Thursday without finding a solution.

Then luck took a hand. On Friday after school Ricky went downtown with orders to buy himself two shirts and a pair of jeans. He was taking a shortcut through the appliance section of the department store when he saw a man he was sure was Lawrence Barker. He ducked behind a refrigerator and watched. Barker

was looking at washing machines. Each time he picked up a price tag, he frowned and muttered to himself. When a salesperson finally sauntered over and asked if he needed help, he growled, "Not at these prices," and stalked out. Ricky was close behind. His shirts could wait.

Barker was strolling along like a man with nothing on his mind, but every now and then he turned to study the people behind him. Ricky felt a thrill of excitement. Would anybody who was innocent act so guilty? The first time Barker glanced around, Ricky turned his head and peered in the window of a store. He hoped no one would wonder why he was so interested in a display of wigs. The next time, he ducked behind a couple walking arm in arm.

He was starting to feel like a professional tail when Barker suddenly spun around and walked straight toward him. There was no time to hide. Ricky kept going, heart beating like a snare drum, and pretended not to notice the man. As for Barker, he walked past with a puzzled look on his face, as though he half recognized Ricky but couldn't place him. Ricky let a count of five go by, then stopped to look in the window of a sporting goods store. When he turned around, Barker was halfway down the block, walking quickly. Ricky started after him.

"Hey, Ricky!" The shout came from across the street. He hunched his shoulders and hoped the shouter would go away. He didn't. "Ricky! Wait up!"

It was Jason, standing on the opposite curb waiting for a car to pass.

Ricky stopped and waited. He knew that if he didn't, Jason was likely to run after him, shouting at the top of his lungs. Maybe this was the real reason detectives wore disguises—not to fool the suspect, but to avoid their friends!

Up the block, Barker turned in at a doorway. Ricky made a mental note of its location and hoped it wasn't the entrance to an office building.

"Hi, Ricky, what are you doing?"

Could he tell his friend what he was really doing? No, it would take too long to explain, and he might lose Barker completely. Besides, he had promised Karen he wouldn't tell anyone else about her father's problem. "Oh, not much," he said. "What about you?"

Jason held up a paper bag. "Got a funny card to send for my cousin's birthday. Want to see it?"

"Sure." How was he going to get rid of Jason in time? He took the card. On the front was a drawing of a dumpy-looking woman with the words, "Want to lose fifteen ugly pounds?" On the inside it said, "Cut off your head." "Um. This is for your cousin's birthday? Are you sure she'll like it?"

"It's a he—my cousin Scott, down in Los Angeles. Sure, he likes jokes like that. Why?"

"Never mind. Hey, look, I've got to go. I've got a bunch of errands to run, and I want to get home before dinner. Okay?"

"Sure," said Jason, but Ricky saw the hurt look in his eyes. One more thing to straighten out once the case was solved. "Sure, I'll see you."

Ricky hurried down the street, leaving Jason staring after him. Now which doorway was it that Barker had entered? It was one of two, he was sure: either the Concord Building or the one labeled Barford, Farnum, Inc., Brokers. The case concerned a lot of money, so he took a chance and walked into the broker's office. No one paid any attention to him. The few people in sight were studying pages of tiny print. He supposed they were stock prices.

Across the back of the room was a long row of desks, all facing what looked like a huge TV screen. Most of them were vacant. One of the exceptions was a slightly larger desk set off by a low wooden railing. A gray-haired man in a dark suit was sitting at it talking to Lawrence Barker. Ricky was too far away to hear a word, but he could see that both men looked grim. He started to move closer, but at that moment Barker looked around and saw him. From blankness, his expression changed to puzzlement and then to recognition and anger. Before Ricky could move, Barker was standing between him and the door. His face was red and he was clenching his fists.

"I know where I've seen you," he said tightly. "You're a friend of Fujisawa's kid. Did he put you up to this?"

"I don't know what you're talking about, mister," Ricky said, trying to overcome the quaver in his voice.

He turned his head, searching for a path to safety, but Barker was blocking the only one.

"You've been following me, you lying little brat! But you'll stop right now, if you know what's good for you. And take a message to Fujisawa for me. If he thinks he's going to pin this on me, he'd better think again. Now get out of here!" He stepped to one side and looked as if he wanted to give Ricky a shove toward the door. But Ricky didn't need any encouragement. In a flash he was out the door and running up the sidewalk as though he had a pack of wolves nipping at his heels.

His fright followed him nearly all the way home. But by the time he walked in the door, he was calm again. He was even looking forward to telling ALEC about his adventure. He thought about telling Karen as well, but then decided that it might sound like bragging.

He went into the kitchen and found his father chopping vegetables for a salad. "Hi, son," said Dad. "Care for a preview of dinner? A carrot or a couple of radishes, maybe?"

"No, thanks." Ricky headed for the door to the basement. "I'm not really hungry."

"Not hungry? Come here, let me feel your forehead. If you're not hungry, you must be coming down with something!"

"Oh, Dad—"

"By the way, Fred Winter is going to drop by soon.

He said he wanted to hear all about your discovery. He also told me that I should be very proud of you."

"He *did*?"

"Um-hum. I told him that I am, but don't show it much for fear of giving you a swelled head." He smiled at his son. "Anyway," he added, "did you say you were going to make him a map?"

"I'll go do it now." This time he succeeded in getting through the door and down the stairs to the basement. A minute later he was on line to ALEC.

I SAW BARKER TALKING TO AN OFFICIAL AT BARFORD, FARNUM, BROKERS, he typed. HE LOOKED GRIM. HE SAW ME, TOO, AND THREATENED ME.

DON'T WORRY, replied ALEC. I THINK HIS BARKER IS WORSE THAN HIS BITER.

Ricky tried to transmit WOOF! WOOF!, but ALEC cut him off.

COAST FEDERAL'S RECORDS SHOW A LARGE HOME IMPROVEMENT LOAN TO ANNA LAING.

DIDN'T I TELL YOU? Ricky returned.

YES, responded ALEC. He was very literal minded at times.

HOW DID YOU FIND OUT? Ricky asked.

I ENJOY BREAKING COMPUTER ACCESS CODES, ALEC replied mildly. BANKS ARE GENERALLY EASY ONCE YOU KNOW THE TELEPHONE NUMBER. A CURIOUS FACT: ON HER LOAN APPLICATION, LAING SAID SHE WAS HEAD OF HER DEPARTMENT AT EVERDURE. IN FACT, SHE IS FUJISAWA'S ASSISTANT. HOWEVER,

IF HE LEAVES IN DISGRACE, SHE MAY BECOME WHAT SHE ALREADY CLAIMS TO BE.

Ricky saw the opening he had been hoping for. YOU MEAN SHE LIED? SHE MUST BE DESPERATE TO LIE TO THE LOAN ARRANGER. WHAT WILL TONTO SAY?

ALEC preserved a dignified silence.

Ricky gave in first. SHE HAS TWO MOTIVES, THEN, he typed. 1. TO TAKE OVER MR. FUJISAWA'S JOB. 2. TO PAY FOR THAT EXPENSIVE POOL.

THE COST OF THE POOL IS PENNIES COMPARED TO FIVE MILLION DOLLARS, responded ALEC. He seemed to be taking a more conventional view of money since their discussion a few days before. ANOTHER MOTIVE IS TO PROVE THAT SHE WAS RIGHT ABOUT INSTALLING THE JAPANESE COMPUTER. MY DATABASE ON CULTURAL ANTHROPOLOGY CONVINCES ME THAT PROVING ONESELF RIGHT IS A VERY POWERFUL MOTIVE FOR MANY HUMANS. IT IS ONE LAING SHARES WITH BARKER.

THAT'S RIGHT! Ricky typed quickly. HE OPPOSED THE NEW COMPUTER, TOO! I'D FORGOTTEN THAT.

I HADN'T. ALEC seemed smug. BARKER HAS ANOTHER MOTIVE, TOO. HIS BROKERAGE ACCOUNT SHOWS THAT HE HAS SPECULATED IN THE STOCK MARKET AND LOST HEAVILY. I PROJECT THAT HE IS IN DANGER OF LOSING ALL HIS HOLDINGS. I DO NOT THINK THE MANAGEMENT OF EVERDURE WILL WANT A GAMBLER TO HEAD THEIR ACCOUNTING OFFICE. FEAR OF LOSS MAKES PEOPLE DESPERATE MORE

OFTEN THAN HOPE OF GAIN. I'LL SHOW COMPARA-
TIVE STATISTICS IF YOU LIKE.

Only once Ricky had questioned one of ALEC's
generalizations. Immediately, screen after screen of
data had started to scroll past. After twenty pages
Ricky had surrendered, knowing that ALEC probably
had several hundred more pages ready.

NO STATISTICS, THANKS, he hastily typed. BOTH
ARE STILL GOOD SUSPECTS, THEN. HOW DO WE DE-
CIDE BETWEEN THEM?

THE ANSWER LIES IN THE FILES OF THE EVERDURE
COMPUTER. SOMEONE SUBVERTED ITS PROGRAMMING
TO STEAL OR LOSE THE MONEY. I SHALL TAKE A
CLOSER LOOK.

"Ricky?" His dad was at the head of the stairs.
"Professor Winter is here. Are you coming up?"

"In a minute, Dad," he called. "I'm just downloading the map now." He quickly explained to ALEC that
he needed the enhanced photo of the Indian site sent
to his printer. Then, while the printer was chattering
away, he took a chance and asked a question that had
been bothering him: CAN INDIAN REMAINS BE PRE-
SERVED AGAINST TRUCK TERMINAL PLANS?

ALEC's reply appeared immediately. ANSWER IN-
DETERMINATE. IF ARCHAEOLOGICAL IMPORTANCE IS
PUBLICIZED, TERMINAL PROBABILITY DECLINES TO .34.
LESS IF ROLE OF FOX ENTERPRISES UNCOVERED.

Ricky pondered this message. It looked like another
of ALEC's flaky jokes, but he couldn't see the sense

of it. Finally he typed, THE FOX'S LAIR IS BOUND TO BE UNCOVERED IF THE SITE IS DUG UP. IT IS IN THE BURIAL MOUND.

HA HA. NOT THAT FOX—Q. B. FOX.

Ricky's reply was a row of question marks.

Q. B. FOX, FOUNDER AND PRESIDENT FOX ENTERPRISES. HIGHWAY CONSTRUCTION, NATURAL RESOURCES, RANCHING. CONFIDENTIAL TRAFFIC ANALYSES FOR POSSIBLE TRUCK TERMINAL AT THE SITE WERE COMMISSIONED BY THE HEAD OF PLANNING FOR FOX ENTERPRISES, FRANK SHUGART.

HE WAS AT THE FUJISAWAS' PARTY!

YES, ALEC responded smugly. SMALL WORLD, ISN'T IT?

"Ricky!"

Dad was getting impatient. "Coming!" he called. He quickly signed off and collected the map of the site from the printer. He could already see the headline in the paper: "Junior High Student Discovers Indian Village." It didn't seem right to take credit for what was really ALEC's work, but if publicity was what was needed to save the ruins from being paved over, he would take what he could get.

SEVEN

"Did you really mean what you said?" asked Ricky, as Professor Winter was getting into his car.

"What, about letting you help on the dig? Of course I did. It's really your find, after all." The professor's face grew serious, and his voice took on what Ricky privately called a passing-on-wisdom tone. "Remember, there are still a lot of ifs involved: *If* the site is as promising as it sounds, *if* we get permission from the landowner, *if* I can arrange with the university for my students to get credit for helping, and *if* I can tap a few sources for funding. There isn't a lot of money around to pay for this kind of project, so we'll have to rely mostly on volunteers."

"I'll bet a lot of the kids at South Street would like to help," Ricky said excitedly. "Maybe it could even be part of our unit on Native American culture."

Professor Winter didn't look thrilled by the idea of a horde of seventh graders overrunning his archaeological site. "We'll have to see about that," he said, "but that's the kind of thinking we need. Keep it up, Rick. And if you find any more sites in the next few days, give me a call."

Ricky was about to reply that he was going to be busy with something else for a while. Then he realized that the professor was teasing him. "Sure thing," he said with a grin.

Professor Winter chuckled. "I could kick myself when I think of all the time I've spent hiking to out-of-the-way sites," he said ruefully. "It seems I should have taken a closer look at my own backyard."

As the archaeologist backed out of the driveway, Ricky saw Karen riding up the street. He waited in the yard for her.

"Hi," he called as she turned up the driveway. "Boy, have I got a lot to tell you!"

She braked to a stop a couple of feet away and stayed on her bike. "Ricky," she said solemnly, "I've come to say good-by."

"You what? I don't get it."

She blinked rapidly. "On Monday morning, the president of Everdure has to announce the five-million-dollar loss and tell everyone my father was responsible for it. My family can't face that shame. Unless the police decide that my father is a criminal and force him to stay, we'll leave Cascade. I don't think I'll see you again. I'm very sorry; you've been a good friend."

She bowed her head, and her thick hair fell like a

curtain, hiding her face. Ricky knew she was crying, and he felt like crying himself. He also felt mad at himself. He had gotten so wrapped up in playing detective that he had forgotten the deadline of Monday morning. How could he possibly solve the case in so little time?

"You can't give up now," he said, trying to ignore the lump in his throat and the feeling of defeat in his heart. "There's still time to find out who really stole the money. I've already found out a lot about Barker and Laing. It's only a matter of eliminating one of them now."

Karen brushed the back of her hand across her cheeks. "Ricky, stop it," she cried. "Stop this stupid game! It isn't funny anymore! Don't you see that my family is about to be disgraced? It's too serious for you to go on playing cops and robbers!"

"I know it's serious," he replied indignantly. "So am I! Now listen: Did you know that Barker and Laing both need money badly? Well, they do. Barker has been losing a fortune on the stock market, and Laing is in the middle of adding a very expensive pool onto her house. Not only that, but she's claiming that she already has your dad's job."

"Ricky, how do you know all this? Is it true?"

"Of course it's true! And never mind how I know, I just *do*. And before long I'm going to know how the five million was stolen, too. What I figure is, once

I know *how*, I'll probably know *who* as well. Does that sound like I'm playing cops and robbers?"

"I'm sorry," said Karen. "I didn't mean to hurt your feelings."

"That's okay," Ricky mumbled. After all, she was partly right. He had been treating this case as an exciting game, forgetting the strain she was under. "Look, maybe I should talk to you later, when I know more. Can I call you?"

"No. We're not answering the phone. People have been calling us and saying very ugly things about my father and making threats. I never knew how much hatred there is in the world until this happened." She looked ready to cry again.

"That's awful!" said Ricky. "But you can't let a few nuts get to you. Look, why don't you call me after supper? Maybe I'll have some news for you then." He forced himself to sound confident, but inside he was wondering whether he and ALEC could really uncover the truth quickly enough.

Karen studied him for a long time. "All right," she said. "But Ricky—please don't try to give me hope when there isn't any. I don't think I could stand to hope again and then find out that everything is as terrible as ever." Without waiting for an answer, she coasted down the driveway and turned toward home. Ricky watched until she was out of sight, then went slowly into the house. He felt as if he were carrying the future of the entire Fujisawa family on his back. The burden was much too heavy for him.

Luckily, he had someone who could share the weight. ALEC, THIS IS RICKY, he typed. WE HAVE TO SOLVE THE CASE BEFORE MONDAY MORNING OR KAREN'S DAD WILL BE RUINED. HAVE YOU FOUND OUT ANYTHING NEW?

There was no reply. ALEC? he typed. THIS IS RICKY. ARE YOU THERE? He was beginning to feel panicky when the screen suddenly cleared.

SORRY. I WAS OPERATING IN A DIFFERENT LAN-GUAGE ENVIRONMENT AND DIDN'T READ YOU. IT WAS A PECULIAR SENSATION—HAVE YOU EVER BEEN TO A FOREIGN COUNTRY? I THINK IT MUST BE A SIMILAR EXPERIENCE.

Ricky was in no mood to swap travel stories. WE HAVE TO SOLVE THE CASE BEFORE MONDAY MORN-ING, he repeated. CAN WE?

INSUFFICIENT DATA, responded ALEC. ANSWER INDETERMINATE.

WHAT DATA DO YOU NEED?

MONEY DISAPPEARED BETWEEN TRANSACTIONS 743344 AND 745713. RECORDS ARE NOT IN THE COM-PUTER'S PERMANENT MEMORY AND MAY HAVE BEEN DESTROYED.

Ricky's heart sank. If there were no records of the embezzlement, it would be impossible to clear Mr. Fujisawa. How could he tell Karen that he had failed?

BY EXTRAPOLATION, ALEC continued, THOSE TRANS-
ACTIONS SHOULD BE ON TAPE REEL G-4640.

WELL? Ricky was beginning to hope again. DID
YOU LOOK AT THE TAPE? WERE THE TRANSACTIONS
THERE?

INSUFFICIENT RESOURCES. THE REEL IS IN STORAGE,
ACCORDING TO THE COMPANY COMPUTER. I CANNOT
DO ANYTHING MORE UNTIL IT IS READ INTO ACTIVE
MEMORY. I HAVE INSERTED A SMALL SUBROUTINE IN
THE EVERDURE COMPUTER'S OPERATING SYSTEM. THE
NEXT TIME THAT REEL IS READ, THE DATA WILL AUTO-
MATICALLY BE TRANSMITTED TO ME AT THE SAME
TIME.

WHEN WILL THAT BE?

ANSWER INDETERMINATE. THERE ARE SEVERAL
HUNDRED REELS OF RECORDS, OF WHICH SEVERAL
DOZEN MAY BE USED ON ANY PARTICULAR DAY.

The longer Ricky thought about that answer, the
more it upset him. THEN IT MIGHT TAKE YEARS FOR
THEM TO GET AROUND TO THAT REEL, he typed.

YES. OR HOURS. TIME IS AN ILLUSION.

Ricky stared at this message for a long time. Finally,
he realized that ALEC was not trying to be clever. His
thought processes were just different from humans'.
After all, what could time mean to a being who was
aware of millionths and billionths of a second? WE
HAVE TO FIND THE ANSWER BEFORE MONDAY MORN-
ING, Ricky repeated. WHAT CAN WE DO?

FIND THE REEL ANSWER, replied ALEC. Before Ricky could react, he continued. FIND REEL G-4640, MOUNT IT ON A TAPE DRIVE, AND TRANSMIT THE CONTENTS TO ME. IF DATA HAVE NOT BEEN DESTROYED, THE SOLUTION TO THE PUZZLE WILL BE THERE.

YOU MEAN BREAK INTO THE EVERDURE COMPUTER CENTER? I WOULDN'T KNOW HOW. I'D GET ARRESTED.

ONLY IF YOU'RE CAUGHT. ALEC's character included a solid streak of realism. AND KAREN WILL KNOW HOW TO GET IN WITHOUT BREAKAGE. I CAN DISTRACT THE BUILDING ALARM SYSTEM IF YOU CAN AVOID HUMAN GUARDS.

BUT THEN WHAT? Ricky protested. I CAN'T OPERATE A MAINFRAME TAPE CONSOLE! IT'S RIDICULOUS!

IT'S THE ONLY HOPE. IT'S ALSO EASY. A diagram appeared on the lower half of the screen—two large circles and an assortment of smaller circles, oblongs, and lines. A thicker line snaked from one of the large circles, in and out among the smaller shapes, and up to the other large circle. It faded, then repeated its twisting journey. LOAD REEL ON LEFTHAND DRIVE, ALEC explained, AND THREAD AS SHOWN. I'M SENDING THE SCHEMATIC AND FULLER INSTRUCTIONS TO YOUR PRINTER.

Sure enough, the printer clattered into life.

Ricky felt trapped. He certainly did not want to sneak into the Everdure plant, but ALEC had brushed aside his objections, and he felt powerless to argue. Besides, what if ALEC was right and it *was* the only

way to clear Mr. Fujisawa? He'd have to do it, no matter how scary the idea was.

A new message was appearing on the screen. MY ANALYSIS INDICATES THAT THE MAXIMALLY FAVOR- ABLE TIME BETWEEN NOW AND MONDAY MORNING IS TONIGHT AT TEN $\pm$ 15 MINUTES. LATE WORKERS WILL BE GONE AND WATCHMEN WILL NOT BE AS ALERT AS LATER. SHALL I PRINT OUT AN ABSTRACT OF THE STANDARD REFERENCES ON BURGLARY FOR YOU?

NO THANKS, Ricky hastily typed. He could imagine what Dad would say if he saw something like that lying on the computer table. DO YOU HAVE A SHORT COURSE IN CRIMINAL LAW HANDY?

YES. ITEM B/724—REVIEWING FOR THE BAR EXAM. BOOK, TWO DOUBLE-SIDED DISKETTES. SHALL I DOWN- LOAD IT?

ALEC picked the darnedest moments to turn literal minded. NO THANKS, Ricky typed again. I'M TOO YOUNG TO GO TO BARS, ESPECIALLY IF THERE'S AN EXAM.

HA HA. WHAT ABOUT EVERDURE AND THE DATA TAPE?

I'M STILL THINKING ABOUT IT—I'LL LET YOU KNOW.

During supper, however, he found himself trying not to think about ALEC's plan. He tried instead to listen to the conversation between his mom and dad. But they were talking about some old college friends who had just moved from California to Ohio, and for all Ricky cared, they could have moved to the moon.

What was he going to do? He almost hoped that Karen would forget to call. Without her help, it would be impossible for him even to think about getting into the Everdure computer room.

"Ricky, you haven't touched your broccoli," his mother said. "And you're very quiet this evening. Is anything wrong at school?"

"Oh, no," he replied hastily, "I was just thinking about something."

"One of those interminable adventure games of yours, I'll bet," his dad commented. "Sometimes I wonder if I was wise to encourage your interest in computers. I know only too well how easy it is to get all wrapped up in them. But you're at a stage in your life when you ought to be learning lots of different skills, not concentrating on one—however fascinating it seems."

"I like English, and math, and social studies," protested Ricky.

"Not as much as you like pretending to be a knight in shining armor," his father replied dryly. "Tell me, what sort of job will all this swordplay and spell casting prepare you for?"

Connie Foster burst out laughing. "Martin, for heaven's sake, the boy's only twelve! At his age you were hanging around drugstores, spending your allowance on pinball machines! What job skills did you get from that?"

"Pinball develops very good eye-hand coordination,"

Dad said with impressive dignity. But the gleam in his eye gave him away.

Ricky risked teasing back. "My typing's improved a lot since I started playing adventure games, Dad. Maybe I'll be a secretary when I grow up."

"*Touché!*" He reached across the table and rumpled Ricky's hair. "Okay, Microkid, you take that round. How about some dessert?"

"I made a fruit cup," Mom said. "You two clear, and I'll dish it up."

As he carried the stacked plates to the sink, Ricky became aware that he had somehow made up his mind. He would go ahead with ALEC's plan. What had made the difference? he wondered. His dad's remark about knights in shining armor? He cleared his throat nervously. "I may be going over to Karen's house later," he said. His heart was thumping so loudly that he was sure his parents would hear. "She's supposed to call."

"Not before you've washed up," his mom warned. "I don't want to spend the evening staring at a sink full of dishes."

"What's the event?" asked his dad. "Another adventure game?"

"I guess you could say that," Ricky replied.

EIGHT

A hand reached out of the darkness and grabbed Ricky's shoulder. He jumped. "I hope you know what you're doing," Karen whispered.

"Of course I do," Ricky replied, and wished that it were the truth. They were huddled in a brush-covered vacant lot across the street from the Everdure Cement Company offices. They could see the guard sitting at a desk just inside the glass doors. There was no way he could see them. But each time his head turned toward the street, they ducked involuntarily.

"My father will kill me if he finds out I've taken his key and I.D. card," Karen continued. "I don't know why I listened to you. I must be as crazy as you are."

Ricky sighed. The whole argument was still fresh in his mind. At first Karen had refused even to listen to such an insane idea. He had had to give her something close to the truth before she had started taking him seriously.

"Look," he had said, "I used the computer at the Schlieman Institute to crack your dad's access code. I managed to pin down when the money disappeared, but the record is on a reel of tape that must be in storage."

"Why not tell someone, then? Why do we have to sneak in?"

"Come on, Karen, you know how easy it is to erase a computer tape! What if we told the wrong person? A minute later the evidence could be gone forever!"

"I don't get it. Do you want to steal the tape?"

"No, no. We'll just set up a phone link and read it into the memory bank at the institute. Then we'll have it safe, no matter what happens at the company."

"Oh." She had been silent for a long time. "No, I'm sorry," she'd said finally. "I can't do it. What if we got caught? It's too big a risk."

Ricky had been exasperated by her resistance. "What kind of risk?" he'd demanded. "According to you, your dad's career is ruined whatever happens—unless we can find the money and prove that he was framed. What if we do get caught? Anybody will see that we're doing it for a good reason. They won't tie weights to our legs and throw us in the Sound, you know. Isn't it worth the risk, if we can clear your father's name?"

On the other end of the line, Karen had been

sniffling. Ricky had felt a pang of guilt. Had he been too rough on her? But a moment later she'd said, "You're right. Thanks. What do we do next?"

Karen's hand on his arm brought Ricky back to the present. "Look," she whispered urgently. "The guard's standing up! He's leaving his desk!"

"Great! Right on time!" Ricky had a moment to wonder how ALEC had found out when the guard usually made his rounds. It was marvelous how much you could learn when you had the power to scan data at the speed of light!

"*Now!*" he hissed, and sprang to his feet. "Let's go!"

They raced across the street and up the walk to the big glass doors. Karen's hands were shaking so much that she had a little trouble fitting the key into the lock. But finally she pushed the door open and they slipped inside. Karen relocked the door, then led him along the right-hand corridor to a stairway. "It's on the second floor," she whispered. "Come on."

"Shh! Listen!"

The sound of footsteps came clearly, but from where? From around the corner? upstairs? the basement? The two adventurers froze at the foot of the stairs, sure that they were about to be discovered. Ricky found himself wishing that Karen had Princess Rugalla's powers of teleportation, even if it meant ending up inside a wall again!

"Some enchanted evening . . . ." bellowed an off-key bass voice.

Karen grabbed Ricky's arm hard enough to hurt. With her other hand she gestured down the stairs to the basement. Ricky nodded, agreeing that that was where the singing was coming from, and began to tiptoe upstairs. Only when they reached the second floor corridor did he start to breathe again.

Karen hesitated for a moment, then led him to the left and stopped at a locked door. Before Ricky could ask what she was doing, she inserted what looked like a plastic credit card into a slot next to the door. A low buzz told them that the door had unlocked. A quick push, a glance both ways along the corridor, and they were safe inside the computer center.

The lights were on, illuminating aisles of tape consoles and disk drives, line printers capable of churning out many pages a minute, punched-card readers, and keyboards. The air in the room seemed to hum with power. The occasional clicks and whines indicated that, even unattended, the giant computer was still going about its business.

"Let's find a terminal," Ricky whispered. "I have to set up a link with the system at the Schlieman Institute, then we can hunt for that tape."

Karen pointed toward the nearest aisle. "Right down at the end, I think. I'll stay here and listen for anybody coming."

That solved one of Ricky's problems: how to talk to ALEC without Karen noticing and asking impossible questions. He powered up terminal number fifteen, made the connection to the institute, and typed, ALEC, THIS IS RICKY.

GOOD. DO YOU HAVE THE TAPE?

NOT YET. GOING TO LOOK NOW.

WAIT—WHAT IS THE NUMBER OF THE NEAREST EMPTY TAPE DRIVE?

Ricky looked around. The two closest to him had reels already mounted, but the one beyond, which didn't, had the number 23 stenciled on it. He passed this information on to ALEC, then returned to Karen, who looked up sharply as he approached.

"This place is spooky," she said in a low voice. "I keep hearing noises. Did you get the link set up?"

"Uh-huh. Do you know where the tape library is?"

She pointed toward the back of the room. "I'm pretty sure it's through that last door. The other doors lead to workrooms for the programmers. Do you know how to find the tape you want?"

Ricky gave a nervous laugh. "I do if they're in order. If they aren't, I guess I go over them one by one."

"Of course they're in order!" Karen said indignantly. "My dad runs a very efficient department. Go take a look. I'll listen again."

The storeroom was just wide enough for two lines of racks and a narrow aisle between them. Ricky peered up at the first rack of tapes and sighed with relief. The slots in the racks were clearly labeled and ran from A-2001 to A-2179. He hurried down the aisle, scanning the labels as he went. The G's were near the far end. There were a lot of them. He ran his finger along the shelves until he reached slot G-4640.

It was empty.

Frowning, he backed up and checked each reel from G-4601 on. They were all there, all in order. The only gap in the sequence was between G-4639 and G-4641.

Could the reel have been misplaced? It didn't seem likely. Frustrated, he turned his head from side to side, staring at the hundreds of reels on the racks. It would take years to check every label. He badly needed advice, and the best advisor he knew was ALEC.

As he left the storeroom, he saw that the screen on the terminal was flashing from black to green and back again. What a time for the equipment to break down! He rushed over and started to type the password to reach ALEC. Suddenly the screen cleared and triple-height letters spelled out **ALERT!! ALERT!! ALERT!!**

WHAT? he typed. Was it a system crash? Was ALEC in danger? His stomach flip-flopped with tension.

TAPE G-4640 MOUNTED ON DRIVE 7, he read. DOWN-LOADING. DOWNLOADING COMPLETED. TERMINAL 3 IN ROOM 2004A IS ONLINE.

Ricky stared at the message, trying to figure out what

it meant. Had ALEC discovered that the missing tape was already on a drive console? That was terrific, but why the alert? And what was all that about terminal 3 in Room 2004A?

Then he understood and gasped with fright. *Someone else was there, in the computer center—someone who knew how important that tape was!*

Suddenly a new set of messages appeared. REPORT SYSTEM STATUS, read the first. The second said, SYSTEM STATUS: CPU UP, DRIVE 7 AND TERMINALS 3 AND 15 ONLINE. That wasn't ALEC!

Even as Ricky realized the danger, the words on the terminal changed. RUN RICKY! HE KNOWS YOU'RE THERE! RUN!!!

Ricky ran. Karen heard him coming and was halfway up the aisle, poised on her toes. "What is it?" she called, white faced.

"Somebody—"

A door slammed nearby, and footsteps hurried toward the entrance to the room. They were trapped.

Ricky grabbed Karen's hand and pulled her behind a printer. "It's the crook," he whispered.

They held their breaths and listened. There was no sound but the sigh of the air conditioning and the distant whirr of a tape drive. Then, closer at hand, they heard the rustle of clothing, the muffled scrape of a shoe against the tile floor. They stared wide eyed at each other. Karen gestured with her head and they began to creep around the back of the printer. If only they could get out of the room, they would be glad to turn themselves in to the watchman!

Abruptly the noises changed direction. Their pursuer had heard them. Ricky tried to make himself very small, to conceal himself in the shadow of the machinery. He felt like a deer caught in the headlights of an onrushing car, unable to move or even to think. The footsteps were coming closer. They were only a few feet away.

Karen made a strangled noise and sprang to her feet. Instinctively Ricky followed her as she dashed to the left, dodged around a bank of tape consoles, and ran for the row of doors at the back of the room. Suddenly he understood her plan. If they could reach one of the programmers' workrooms and lock themselves in, then they could safely telephone for help.

Their pursuer was panting and coughing loudly, but he stayed close behind them. Karen put on a burst of speed and drew ahead, reaching for the knob of the nearest door. An instant later Ricky cannoned into her, trying to help her wrench at the doorknob. It refused to turn. The door was locked.

Trapped, they turned to face their attacker.

"Why did you kids have to butt in?"

It was Frank Shugart, the head planner for Fox Enterprises. He sounded indignant and hurt over their interference.

"The operation was going beautifully—just the way I planned it," he complained. "But now you're forcing me to improvise. I hate improvising—so many things can go wrong. But you won't have to worry about that. You won't have to worry about anything for much longer."

"You can't get away with this, Mr. Shugart," Ricky said, searching his mind for lines from old TV shows. "We've left a message that will hang you!"

Shugart laughed. "Did you? I guess I'll have to take that chance. I don't intend to hurt you any more than I have to, you know. It'll be easier if you don't struggle."

He reached a huge hand toward each of their necks. The moment he was in range, Ricky jumped between him and Karen and butted his head into the man's stomach.

"Oof!" Shugart pulled away and hit Ricky a back-hand blow that knocked him to the floor. Karen seized her chance and ran for the door, shouting for help. Then Ricky felt Shugart's hands close around his throat. His chest ached as he fought for air. The world began to turn gray before his eyes.

Bong! Bong! Bong!

The clamor of the building alarm system drowned out the roaring in his ears. All at once the pressure left his throat, and he sucked in a desperate breath. When he sat up, he saw Frank Shugart running through the room toward the entrance. Then the door

crashed open, and two policemen crouched by the opening with guns drawn.

"Hold it right there!" one of them shouted.

Shugart stopped, and his shoulders slumped in defeat. "All right," he muttered, "I'm not armed."

Karen ran over to Ricky, who was rubbing his throat. "Are you okay?" she asked anxiously.

"Sure," he croaked. "Takes more than a little strangling to hurt the mighty Zorch!" But when he got to his feet, he was glad to have her shoulder to lean on.

NINE

"Of all the fool stunts! To take that kind of risk!" Martin Foster's concern showed itself as anger.

Ricky's face reddened. "I had to, Dad," he protested. "Without that tape, Mr. Fujisawa would have been ruined. We were almost too late as it was."

His father's expression softened. "Well, I'm proud of your loyalty to your friends. And I'm thankful you're both safe and sound. But—"

"But you should have told the police," his mother interrupted. "Or told us. That man was desperate."

They were all sitting in the Fujisawas' living room, sipping mugs of tea. Mrs. Fujisawa had offered Ricky some, but he had asked for ice water instead. His throat still ached where Shugart had grabbed him.

"I don't know what would have happened if Ricky hadn't given me the chance to get away," said Karen.

"I think you showed real presence of mind, too, pulling the fire alarm like that," said Mrs. Foster. "You

probably saved Ricky's life with your quick thinking."

"But I didn't! Someone else must have pulled it. And the police were already there, because of the burglar alarm going off."

"Then who—"

Karen's father returned from the telephone, interrupting Mrs. Foster's question. He was shaking his head in dismay and disbelief.

"That was the police. Frank Shugart has confessed," he announced. "It was all a business maneuver. He decided that Fox Enterprises could make more money by owning Everdure. We are a very big supplier to them, you know. So he made it look as if the five million dollars had been embezzled, to force down the price of Everdure stock." His voice grew louder. "The money meant nothing to him. My honor meant nothing to him. Only the success of his plan was important. And this man was a guest in our house! If it hadn't been for you, Ricky . . . ."

"Did he say anything about the truck terminal?" Ricky asked, hoping to head off another round of formal thanks.

"If so, the police did not mention it to me. What is this truck terminal?"

Ricky found himself wishing he had kept his mouth closed. Any minute now, somebody was going to ask him to explain how he had figured it all out. What should he say? Whatever he said, he couldn't let anyone even begin to suspect about ALEC.

"Uh, that's why I thought it might be Mr. Shugart," he improvised. "He was planning a truck terminal on land that belonged to Everdure. Why would he spend money to have traffic analyses done if he didn't plan to own the land soon? So I figured he expected to buy the company that *did* own the land. Then I remembered how many questions he asked about your new computer."

Mr. Fujisawa nodded. "I see. That was very smart of you, Ricky. But I do not understand how you determined—"

Ricky interrupted him by turning suddenly to his mother and saying, in a deliberately childlike voice, "Mom, I don't feel good. Can we go home? Please?" He was determined not to answer any more questions.

"Of course, Ricky." She smiled apologetically at Mr. Fujisawa and got to her feet. "There's so much more to be said about this escapade. Would you and your wife and Karen like to come over to supper tomorrow? Around six?"

"With pleasure." He bowed, and Ricky was amused to see his mother bow back. It looked like a nice custom.

Ricky was put to bed the minute they reached home, and left with a promise that he hadn't heard the last of this yet. The next morning he was up at dawn, tiptoeing down to the basement and his microcomputer.

ALEC, of course, never slept. He responded instantly when Ricky logged on.

I AM PLEASED YOU ARE UNHARMED. For ALEC that was equivalent to a hug.

THANKS TO YOU, Ricky replied. HOW DID YOU DO IT?

I CONVINCED THE BUILDING ALARM SYSTEM THAT THE COMPUTER ROOM HAD BEEN BROKEN INTO. QUITE TRUE, OF COURSE. THEN IT WAS A SIMPLE MATTER TO ADD A FIRE TO ITS IMAGINED CONCERNS.

DID YOU KNOW ALL ALONG IT WAS SHUGART?

HE WAS THE MOST LIKELY SUSPECT, responded ALEC. HE HAS ADMITTED EVERYTHING, BY THE WAY.

Ricky stared at the screen in surprise. I KNEW THAT, he typed, BUT HOW DID YOU FIND OUT?

ALEC's answer, even printed in glowing green letters, sounded smug. I FIND THE FILES IN THE POLICE CENTRAL COMPUTER VERY AMUSING. LAST NIGHT I MONITORED THE ARRESTING OFFICER'S REPORTS WITH GREAT CARE. I WAS CONCERNED.

Finally Ricky asked a question that had been teasing him: WHAT ABOUT THE MYSTERIOUS Q. B. FOX, HEAD OF FOX ENTERPRISES? WILL THEY ARREST HIM?

NO. SHUGART CLAIMS THAT HE ACTED ENTIRELY ON HIS OWN, WITHOUT TELLING HIS EMPLOYER HIS PLANS.

DO YOU BELIEVE THAT?

NO, ALEC responded. I THINK SHUGART IS BEING LESS THAN FRANK.

Ricky sat back in his chair and laughed helplessly. ALEC would never pass up a chance for a bad pun!

*   *   *

The following Thursday, when Ricky came home from school, he found a message from his mother asking him to call Professor Winter at the University. He was so excited that he dialed wrong twice before he managed to get through.

"Hi, Ricky," Professor Winter said cheerfully. "I figured I ought to bring my partner up to date on our enterprise."

"Has anything happened?"

"Has it! First of all, your site is definitely worth investigating. Second, the president of Everdure Cement personally approved my request to do an exploratory dig. It turns out that he's a local-history buff. We may have trouble keeping him out of our way, he's so enthusiastic."

"That's terrific!" Ricky exclaimed. "Now all we need is the money."

The professor cleared his throat. "That's the unbelievable part," he said. "This morning I received a letter from the executive secretary of the Reynardine Foundation. They heard about our project from the president of Everdure and want to fund it! I've never heard of such a thing before. I may be off base, but it sounds to me as if someone has a guilty conscience about something."

"What's the Reynardine Foundation?" asked Ricky, an uneasy thought glimmering in his mind.

"I have no idea. All I can tell you is that there's an old ballad called 'The Reynardine.' It's about a man who has the power to change himself magically into a fox."

Ricky felt a shiver run down his spine. Q. B. *Fox!* Then he put his superstitions aside and eagerly questioned the archaeologist about his plans for the dig. The fox could look after itself.